THE hm STUDY SKILLS PROGRAM

WORKSHOP LEADER'S
HANDBOOK

Module Three: For The hm Study Skills Program, Level II
Grades 8–10

Developed by **hm:** The Study Skills Group

Authors: Dana Martin-Newman, Ed.D.

Amie Watson, Ed.D.

Senior Editor: David Marshak

Editors: Kiyo Morimoto, Director
Bureau of Study Counsel
Harvard University

Jerome A. Pieh, Headmaster
Milton Academy

The National Association of Secondary School Principals
Reston, Virginia 22091

ISBN 0-88210-169-2

Materials:

1. Transparencies 1, 2, 3 (found on pages 22-24)
2. *hm Student Text, Level II* — one per participant
3. *hm Teacher's Guide, Level II* — one per participant
4. Pencil — one per participant
5. Writing paper
6. Chalk and chalkboard
7. Blank transparencies — one per group
8. Overhead (OH) pens — one per group
9. Tissue or wet sponge — one per group
10. Overhead projector and screen

* *

> **Make sure participants have a copy of the**
> **_Teacher's Guide_ and _Student Text_ for _Level II_.**

Objectives of the Workshop:

By the end of this Workshop you will have accomplished four objectives:

1. You will have sampled two units from the *hm Study Skills Program, Level II.*

2. You will have reviewed some teaching suggestions for those two sample units.

3. You will have reviewed the *hm Study Skills Program, Level II* and will be familiar with its contents, organization, and teaching suggestions.

4. You will have been introduced to the *hm Level II Teacher's Guide* and *Student Text.*

Sample Unit:
Note Taking Methods, Unit III
Student Text, pg. 18
Teacher's Guide, pg. 23

Effective note taking is perhaps the single most useful study skill that a student can learn. The process of taking notes results in learning both when the notes are *taken* and when they are *used*.

This unit presents two note taking methods: (1) **outlining**; and (2) **mapping**. These two methods are introduced through their application to written materials.

To take notes effectively, students must have the ability to identify main ideas and important details within a written or oral presentation. It is assumed here that your students have already developed at least a rudimentary skill in identifying main ideas and details. If many or some of your students do not have this skill yet, we suggest that you provide them with the necessary instruction before teaching this unit. You can find an example of this kind of instruction in the *hm Study Skills Program, Level I* in Unit IX.

Now we will sample Unit III from the *hm Study Skills Program, Level II* by actively participating as students in the instruction. Please role-play a student in your class.

"Why Take Notes?"
pg. 18

Please read to yourself "Why Take Notes?" on page 18 of your *Student Text* and find out the purposes of note taking.

Allow reading time.

What are the purposes of note taking? What does the concept of note taking involve?

Allow discussion time.

We will show you two effective ways of taking notes: **outlining** and **mapping.** Try using both of them before you judge them, and discover how well they work for you.

"Outlining"
pg. 19

Read "Outlining" and "Paragraph I" on page 19.

Allow reading time.

"Outline For Paragraph I"
pg. 19

Recall the main ideas and important data from "Paragraph I." Then, read the "Outline for Paragraph I" on page 19, and compare your main ideas and details with the ones given in the "Outline for Paragraph I."

Are there any other ideas/facts and/or details that you would add to the "Outline For Paragraph I?"

"How To Outline"
"Outline Form"
"Tips For Taking Notes"
pg. 20

Now let's read page 20 in your *Student Text:* "How To Outline," "Outline Form," and "Tips For Taking Notes." Then, complete Exercise I on page 21, writing on paper or in your *hm* book.

Exercise I
pg. 21

Are there volunteers who would be willing to write their Exercise I outlines on the chalkboard?

As you can see, outlining is a *personal* study skill. Although the outline form is the same, the wording and placement of data are individual.

"Mapping"
pg. 22

Mapping is another note taking method, an alternative method that can be useful: (1) to students for whom outlining is not a helpful tool; and (2) in situations where the presentation lacks a clear organization, such as a discussion. Mapping requires a less sequential organization than outlining yet results in nearly equally well-organized notes. Although mapping may be new to you, we suggest that you examine it carefully and experiment with it for its many uses.

Read "Mapping" and "Paragraph II" on page 22 to yourselves.

Allow reading time.

Are there any other ideas/facts and/or details that you would add to the "Map For Paragraph II?"

Allow discussion time.

"How To Map"
pg. 23

Read "How To Map" on page 23, and then complete Exercise II.

Exercise II
pg. 23

Allow working time.

Are there volunteers, preferably those who did not do outlining on the chalkboard, who would write their mapping notes on the chalkboard?

Ask volunteers to write their mapping on the chalkboard.

Allow discussion time.

As you can see, mapping is also a *personal* study skill, using an individual's own ideas/facts and details. Both mapping and outlining are useful tools for achieving the same purpose: taking personally meaningful and useful notes.

Exercise III
pgs. 24-25

Exercise III on page 24 asks you to map several paragraphs, putting supporting details in sequence. Read the directions for Exercise III.

```
Allow reading time.
```

Are there any questions?

```
Allow questioning time.
```

You can write in the *hm* book or on your own paper. Try mapping in sequence the first three paragraphs.

```
Allow working time.
```

Was this exercise more difficult than not sequencing when mapping?

Do you think your comprehension was greater because of the sequencing?

Would it be easier for you to map/sequence when listening rather than reading?

```
Elicit responses.

Allow discussion time.
```

"Using Abbreviations and
Symbols In Note Taking"
pg. 26

One good way to save time when you are taking notes is to use *abbreviations* and *symbols* whenever possible.

Read page 26 and do Exercise IV.

6

Exercise IV.
pg. 26

Give me three different symbols or abbreviations for each word in Exercise III. I'll write them on the chalkboard.

Discuss the following questions:

1. Where do you think your students would have difficulty with this note taking unit?

2. How would you introduce this unit to your students, and how would you build upon it using your own curriculum?

3. How would you integrate these note taking activities into your curriculum?

"Taking Useful Notes"
pg. 27

"Taking Useful Notes," page 27, is an overview of the importance of taking your own **personal** notes — notes you feel comfortable using.

"Summary"
pg. 27

Please read the "Summary" on page 27.

1. How does taking notes help you to learn?

2. What are two good methods for taking notes?

In sampling "Note Taking Methods," we have engaged in whole class and individual instruction in an active, participatory way. We learn by doing, we learn by practice, and we learn in cooperation with our peers.

The *hm Study Skills Program, Level II* is a starting point, a kick-off place to study skills learning, a way to help students learn how to learn more efficiently by applying study skills.

After teaching this unit, a teacher should provide students with varied opportunities to practice these newly developed skills. Through **practice**, using classroom curriculum, students will be better able to master these study skills and apply them to other learning situations.

Show Transparency 1.

Students can become more effective, independent learners and become more aware of how best they learn by **learning-by-doing**. **Learning-by-doing** is a prerequisite for becoming a disciplined, self-esteemed, independent learner, designing, orchestrating, monitoring, evaluating, and deciding what skills and activities are most effective for a particular learning situation.

As students gain awareness of the value of study skills, they become more motivated to learn them, to become skilled learners. And the more competent and skillful they become, the more confident they grow in their ability to learn. So, in successful, **learning-by-doing**, students simultaneously generate study skills and increased self-esteem and self-discipline. This is the upward spiral of success generated by increasing competence and confidence.

Sample Unit:
A Way To Read Textbooks, Unit V
Student Text, pg. 33
Teacher's Guide, pg. 28

This unit offers students a way to experience textbook reading as a challenge, as an activity that can earn their interest and involvement. To this end, this unit presents a method for learning from textbooks and engages students in an initial practice of its use. This method includes three steps: (1) surveying; (2) reading and taking notes; and (3) reviewing.

Let's organize ourselves into small groups, three to four in each group, with the members of each group sitting together.

We recommend that this unit be taught in small groups to encourage interaction and active involvement. Students will be encouraged to share the work of the group actively, even if it seems inefficient at times. Then, after the initial lessons, you will want to structure assignments on an individual basis.

Allow group formation time.

"Introduction"
pg. 33

Please read the "Introduction" on page 33 of your *Student Text*, and respond to Exercise I either on your paper or in your *hm* book. Remember that you are role-playing one of your students as you do these activities.

Allow working time.

How are textbooks different from novels and stories? I'll list your answers on the chalkboard.

Elicit answers.

"How Do You Read A Textbook?"
"A Way To Read Textbooks"
pgs. 33-34

Read to yourselves "How Do You Read A Textbook?" and "A Way To Read Textbooks," pages 33-34.

Allow reading time.

Now let's discuss each step of the **Three Step Method.**

What does it mean to **survey** your assignment before you start to read?

Allow discussion time.

Ask a volunteer to answer question.

Answers:

1. Read chapter titles.
2. Read introduction and section headings.
3. Read summary paragraphs.
4. Read review questions.

After surveying your textbook, the next step is to **read** it and to decide if you want to **take notes.** If you want to **take notes,** what method would you choose? How does that method coincide with your own learning style?

Elicit responses.

The third and last step is to **review** — to go over the main ideas and important details you have just read. What are some ways you can **review**?

Elicit responses.

Answers:

1. Talking it over with a friend.
2. Re-reading your notes.
3. Talking it over in a group.
4. Asking and answering questions from what you have just read.

What do you know about your own reviewing methods? Do they coincide with what you now know about your learning style?

Allow discussion time.

One good way to **review,** whether by yourself or with a friend or friends, is to ask and answer questions. You can: (1) turn each heading and/or subheading into a question and try to answer it; (2) ask "how," "what," "why," and/or "who"; and (3) answer the "questions for study" at the end of the chapter(s).

Exercise II
pgs. 35-36

Now let's try out our **Three Step Method** knowledge on Exercise II, pages 35-36. You may write in the *hm* book or on a piece of paper. Do this exercise as a group effort, producing one answer for each group. I will then ask for a volunteer to write her/his answer on the chalkboard.

```
┌──────────────────────────────────────────────┐
│                                                │
│            Allow working time.                 │
│                                                │
└──────────────────────────────────────────────┘
```

```
┌──────────────────────────────────────────────┐
│                                                │
│          Ask a volunteer to write answer       │
│              on the chalkboard.                 │
│                                                │
└──────────────────────────────────────────────┘
```

```
┌──────────────────────────────────────────────┐
│                                                │
│           Allow discussion time.               │
│                                                │
└──────────────────────────────────────────────┘
```

"What Are The Advantages Of The Survey, Read And Take Notes, Review Method?"
pg. 37

"Tips For Taking Notes From Your Reading"
pg. 38

Read to yourselves "What Are The Advantages Of The Survey, Read And Take Notes, Review Method?" and "Tips For Taking Notes From Your Reading" on pages 37 and 38.

```
┌──────────────────────────────────────────────┐
│                                                │
│            Allow reading time.                 │
│                                                │
└──────────────────────────────────────────────┘
```

```
┌──────────────────────────────────────────────┐
│                                                │
│     Distribute transparencies, pens, and tissues. │
│                                                │
└──────────────────────────────────────────────┘
```

Exercise III
pgs. 38-39

Exercise III on pages 38 and 39 will also be a group effort. You will have 15 minutes to complete the exercise, so organize yourselves. One answer per group. Have one person write the group answer on a blank transparency. We will go over your answers and critique them.

Allow working time.

Now let's discuss each group's answer.

**Have each group show its transparency
on the screen.
Invite people to discuss each group's work.**

Did each group have the important facts and details? Did each group use the same note taking methods?

Allow discussion time.

"Summary"
pg. 39

Please read the "Summary" on page 39.

Allow reading time.

What are the three steps in the **Three Step Method**? What does each step involve?

Elicit responses.

Regardless of what subject or subjects you teach, if textbook reading is part of your curriculum, then taking time to teach the **Three Step Method** should be a beneficial part of your program.

We have just sampled two units from the *hm Study Skills Program, Level II*. Each unit actively involved you with different strategies in small groups, whole class, and individual activities.

Suggestions for using the
*hm Study Skills Program,
Level II*

Now that we have sampled two units, I wish to make several suggestions for using the *hm Program:*

12

1. The *hm Study Skills Program, Level II* is designed to be taught in a classroom. It is not programmed material that a student can work through on her/his own, though some units may be used on an individual basis.

2. Each unit should be taught within an on-going course. These study skills need to be integrated into the regular curriculum for **real** experiences.

3. Once a unit is taught, it needs to be followed up by **practice** within a curriculum, so students see the value of that study skill.

4. Small group, whole class, and individual instruction are suitable for the *hm Study Skills Program, Level II.*

5. **ANY SKILL TAKES MORE TIME TO USE WHEN ONE IS FIRST LEARNING IT. AS COMPETENCE FOLLOWS PRACTICE THE SKILL BECOMES AUTOMATIC!**

Are there any comments about these suggestions?

Allow discussion time.

Introduction to
*hm Study Skills Program,
Level II
Teacher's Guide*

Now let's quickly walk through the *hm Study Skills Program, Level II Teacher's Guide.*

We want you to peruse the *Guide,* become familiar with its format, and feel comfortable with its contents, suggestions, and instructions.

If you have any additions or deletions, please feel free to discuss them here and/or incorporate them into your class lessons.

Table of Contents

In the Table of Contents in your *Teacher's Guide,* the *hm Study Skills Program, Level II* lists twelve units in which students have the opportunity to practice basic study skills. We learn skills by doing, by trial and error, by making independent decisions. These twelve units can give your students varied opportunities to explore and expand their study skills.

The twelve units are:

1. Learning To Listen
2. Vocabulary: Getting Meaning From Context
3. Note Taking Methods
4. Listening And Taking Notes
5. A Way To Read Textbooks
6. Solving Problems
7. How Do You Study?
8. Improving Your Memory
9. Organizing The Paragraph
10. Preparing For And Taking Tests: Objective Questions
11. Preparing For And Taking Tests: Essay Questions
12. Using Your Time

Level II also includes two articles, pages 58-63, which explore the values and uses of study skills as well as ways to organize and teach study skills instruction.

Introduction to the
*hm Study Skills Program:
Level II*
pgs. 1-3

Pages 1-3 give us an "Introduction to the *hm Study Skills Program: Level II*": definitions and history along with the underlying values upon which the *hm Study Skills Program* is based.

These values have been stressed when we sampled our two units and will be emphasized more when we peruse the *Teacher's Guide* and *Student Text.*

The *hm Study Skills Program,
Level II*
pg. 2

Page 2 in your *Teacher's Guide* addresses the fact that each of the *hm Study Skills Program, Level II* units focuses on students who:

1. Have a combination of a lack of skills and a minimum of self-confidence, and who need an introduction to a skill.

2. Have begun to develop study skills but have not learned to organize these skills into an efficient system for mastery.

3. Are doing well but need help in developing more efficient study skills review and reinforcement.

Each unit allows for the active participation of students who have a diversity of skills and levels of competence.

Quickly read this "Introduction" section, pages 1-3.

Teaching the *hm Study Skills Program, Level II:*
A Discussion Of Means And Ends
pgs. 4-10

Page 4 states that your teaching of the *hm Study Skills Program, Level II* should incorporate repeated **practice**, usable feedback, rewards, and reasonable levels of expected mastery for each unit. It is important to provide students with the opportunity to make mistakes and try again in learning study skills, without the feeling that they have failed. Also, it is important to inform your students at the beginning of their use of the *hm Program* about how they will be evaluated.

Are there any questions about what this would actually involve in the classroom?

Allow discussion time.

Study Skills And Learning Styles

Where To Teach The
hm Study Skills Program

Building Study Skills Instruction
Into The Curriculum
pg. 5

Page 5 emphasizes that:

(1) Teaching of study skills be guided by an awareness of individual differences in students' learning style, whereby students learn more about their own learning style while learning specific study skills;

(2) *Level II* can be successfully taught within the context of any subject with the exception, perhaps, of mathematics (see *hm Math Study Skills*);

(3) *Level II* should be taught within the context of an already existing course to help students see both the immediate and long-term value of mastering and using study skills.

Pacing Of The *hm*
Program, Level II
pg. 6

Page 6 recommends possible organizations or pacings for the teaching of the units in *Level II:*

1. Within a subject area or self-contained class, one unit per week over a twelve week period.

2. A division of the instructional load among different subject area teachers, with each one teaching some part of the *hm Program.*

3. Within a subject area or self-contained class, three-four units in a one month period; then, a second month for on-going practice, followed by the use of another three-four units in a one month period; and so on.

4. Within a subject area or self-contained class, one unit every three-four weeks over the length of most of the school year.

Using Small Groups
In The Classroom
pg. 6

Small group instruction is recommended for many units and activities in the *hm Program,* although individual work is of critical importance for practice after a skill has been introduced.

Small group instruction lets students:

1. Learn study skills through shared problem solving;

2. Share their talents and experiences while learning from each other;

3. Be actively involved with their learning.

When you were working in your small groups, you had two jobs to do: (1) decide how to work together; and (2) have each person first complete worksheets, exercises, practices, etc. individually. You did this automatically, but successful small group instruction takes careful classroom planning.

Using the *hm Study Skills Program:*
Suggested Directions, Suggested
Times, and Unit Summaries
pg. 7

Page 7 lists *suggested* directions and *suggested* times.

"Suggested Directions" are offered for each unit. Please adapt them in ways that are beneficial to you and your students.

16

"Suggested Times" are structured so that each unit fits into a single period. These times are *approximate,* based on a variety of classroom testings. We strongly suggest you gauge your times according to your students' needs and your own teaching style.

"Unit Summaries"
pg. 7

Page 7 explains that each unit includes a "Summary" as its final page, both in the *Teacher's Guide* and *Student Text.* We recommend that you bring these summaries to the attention of your students.

Grading And The *hm*
Study Skills Program
pg. 8

It is suggested that students' involvement with the *hm Program* be graded on a mastery basis — repeated practice over time. Students' grades result not from each practice with a study skill but from the level of mastery that students achieve in that study skill at the end of a certain amount of time.

Teaching The "Introduction"
To The Student Text
pg. 10

The "Introduction," page 10 in the *Teacher's Guide,* introduces the *hm Level II Program* to your students. This material offers them:

1. An initial awareness of what study skills are;

2. An introduction to the value that study skills can bring to them personally;

3. An introduction to the concept of learning style, and a brief exploration of their own style of learning.

Suggested Directions for
the Introduction
pg. 10

"Suggested Directions for the Introduction," page 10, asks that you prepare your students for study skill learning by giving them a brief overview of the *hm Program:* (1) what study skills will be included; (2) time spent on study skill learning; and (3) criteria for study skill grades.

"Suggested Directions for the Introduction" also offers directions for: (1) understanding the concept of learning style, given in the *Student Text* pages 2-3; and (2) instructional strategies of small group discussion and whole class questions and answers.

You have just surveyed this *Teacher's Guide.* For maximum results with the *hm Study Skills Program, Level II,* examine both the *Student Text* and *Teacher's Guide* carefully prior to your coordinating your curriculum with the *hm Study Skills Program.*

Are there any questions? Comments?

Allow discussion time.

"Introduction"
Student Text, pgs. 1-3
Teacher's Guide, pgs. 1-11

Now we will walk through the *Teacher's Guide* and the *Student Text.*

Both the *Teacher's Guide,* pages 1–11, and the *Student Text,* pages 1–3, begin with a study skill and learning style "Introduction." We discussed this "Introduction" extensively during the *Overview* and *Teacher's Guide* sections.

Unit I
Student Text, pg. 4
Teacher's Guide, pg. 11

Please open your *Teacher's Guide* to page 11 and your *Student Text* to page 4.

Allow time to locate pages.

Notice that this unit in the *Teacher's Guide* begins with some background information for the teacher about listening.

"Suggested Directions"
Teacher's Guide, pgs. 11-13

Next, on pages 11–13 in your *Teacher's Guide,* you see a brief set of "Suggested Directions" for teaching the unit.

Unit I, *Student Text,* requires that students respond on page 4 to questions you read to them from page 11 of the *Teacher's Guide.*

"Additional Suggestions"
Teacher's Guide, pgs. 14-15

Pages 14–15 in your *Teacher's Guide* give "Additional Suggestions" that will allow you to extend your students' experiences in listening beyond the activities presented in the *Student Text.*

Unit I: "Summary"
Student Text, pg. 7
Teacher's Guide, pg. 16

Next, on page 16 of your *Teacher's Guide,* is a clear "Summary" of the skills introduced to students in this unit. This matches the unit "Summary" on page 7 of the *Student Text.*

Unit Organization

Unit I of the *Teacher's Guide* is organized typically. All other units follow the same pattern of:

1. Background information for teachers, which appears at the beginning of each unit

2. Suggested Directions for the unit

3. Additional Suggestions

4. Summary.

Many units in the *Student Text* are organized as follows:

1. Introduction — purposes and focus of the unit

2. Exercises

3. Summary.

Other units are organized in a somewhat different way:

1. Exploratory activity

2. Introduction — purposes and focus of the unit

3. Exercises

4. Summary.

Answers

Where appropriate, answers for the exercises are included after the "Suggested Directions." They are clearly marked. What pages in the *Teacher's Guide* contain the answers to Unit II? (pg. 19-20)

Elicit responses.

You can stop here or continue through the remaining units in a similar manner.

Unit II
Student Text, pg. 8
Teacher's Guide, pg. 17

Unit III
Student Text, pg. 18
Teacher's Guide, pg. 23

Unit IV
Student Text, pg. 28
Teacher's Guide, pg. 28

Unit V
Student Text, pg. 33
Teacher's Guide, pg. 30

Unit VI
Student Text, pg. 40
Teacher's Guide, pg. 33

Unit VII
Student Text, pg. 48
Teacher's Guide, pg. 37

Unit VIII
Student Text, pg. 55
Teacher's Guide, pg. 40

Unit IX
Student Text, pg. 65
Teacher's Guide, pg. 45

Unit X
Student Text, pg. 73
Teacher's Guide, pg. 48

Unit XI
Student Text, pg. 85
Teacher's Guide, pg. 52

Unit XII
Student Text, pg. 93
Teacher's Guide, pg. 55

Level II includes two articles in your *Teacher's Guide,* pages 58–63, that acquaint teachers with study skills organizational and instructional strategies.

Closure: Goals

Show Transparency 3.

Now that we have sampled and surveyed two sample units, the *Teacher's Guide,* and *Student Text,* we hope this *hm Study Skills Program, Level II* Training Session has:

1. Focused your attention on study skills as basic skills.

2. Helped you begin to understand the need to organize your teaching of study skills.

3. Shown you ways of actively involving your students in their own learning.

4. Shown you ways of instructing your students in "learning-to-learn."

5. Explored varied study skill methods that can help your students become effective, independent learners.

Questions answered by the *hm Study Skills Program, Level II*

We also hope that the following questions will be answered for you as you become more proficient with the *hm Study Skills Program, Level II:*

1. How can instructional methods be devised to help students learn how to learn?

2. How can students:

   (a) Improve their academic performance?

   (b) Enhance their ability to perform future tasks of the same kind?

   (c) Transfer their knowledge and skills to other subject areas?

3. How can we help students learn to:

   (a) Make independent decisions?

   (b) Listen to directions and follow them accurately?

   (c) Take a test effectively?

Independent Learning

LEARNING BY DOING

1. Designing
2. Orchestrating
3. Monitoring
4. Evaluating
5. Deciding
6. Refining

YOUR BEST STUDY SKILLS

1. Self-Awareness
2. Self-Reward/Esteem
3. Self-Discipline

INDEPENDENT LEARNER/DECISION MAKER WITH STUDY SKILL CHOICES

SUGGESTIONS FOR USING THE
hm STUDY SKILLS PROGRAM, LEVEL II

1. The *hm Study Skills Program, Level II* is designed to be taught in a classroom. It is not programmed material that a student can work through on her/his own, though some units may be used on an individual basis.

2. Each unit should be taught within an on-going curriculum. These study skills need to be integrated into the regular curriculum for **real** experiences.

3. Once a unit is taught, it needs to be followed up by **practice** within a curriculum so students see the value of that study skill.

4. Small group, whole class, and individual instruction are suitable for the *hm Study Skills Program, Level II.*

5. **ANY SKILL TAKES MORE TIME TO USE WHEN ONE IS FIRST LEARNING IT. AS COMPETENCE FOLLOWS PRACTICE, THE SKILL BECOMES AUTOMATIC!**

GOALS

We hope this Training Session has:

(1) Focused your attention on study skills as basic skills.

(2) Helped you begin to understand the need to organize your teaching of study skills.

(3) Shown you ways of actively involving your students in their own learning.

(4) Shown you ways of instructing your students in *learning-to-learn.*

(5) Explored varied study skill methods that can help your students become effective, independent learners.

QUESTIONS ANSWERED BY THE hm STUDY SKILLS PROGRAM

We hope that the following questions will be answered for you as you become more proficient with the *hm Study Skills Program:*

(1) How can instructional methods be devised to help students learn how to learn?

(2) How can students:

    (a) Improve their academic performance?

    (b) Enhance their ability to perform future tasks of the same kind?

    (c) Transfer their knowledge and skills to other subject areas?

(3) How can we help students learn to:

    (a) Make independent decisions?

    (b) Listen to directions and follow them accurately?

    (c) Take a test effectively?